C000138763

EMOTIONS

Daniel Townsend

Grosvenor House
Publishing Limited

This book is published by
Grosvenor House Publishing Ltd
Link House
140 The Broadway, Tolworth, Surrey, KT6 7HT.
www.grosvenorhousepublishing.co.uk

A CIP record for this book
is available from the British Library

ISBN 978-1-83975-855-3

Dedicated to my friends and family and all those who believed in me and encouraged me to begin this journey.

I write from my heart and soul very openly and honestly hoping to reach those who need to feel less alone and understood.

Preface

As this is my first book I have put years of work into it and have gone on a very deep and personal journey. I hope it's meaning reaches the reader and they can relate and feel less alone and more understood. That would be the greatest reward.

Thoughts

If my thoughts could speak
how would they sound?
Would they be quiet or
would they be loud?
Would they convey
all I want to say?
Would they be mumbled,
or would they be clear
and make sense to those who hear?
Would I be noticed and would people care
if my thoughts could speak and be
laid bare.

Have you ever?

Have you ever felt lost
not knowing where to turn?
Have you ever felt alone
even in a crowded room?
Have you ever felt not good
enough or even just okay?
Have you ever felt that every day
would all just be the same?
Have you ever felt trapped
all because of fear?
Have you ever felt you
didn't want to be here?
Have you ever felt misunderstood
and that you are judged?
Have you ever felt alone and
unworthy of love?
I promise you right now
that you aren't alone.
That many of us have been
there too and we felt the same I know.

So lonely

Have you ever felt so lonely
you thought you'd disappear?
Because nobody sees you,
were you even here?
Having only yourself
as company every single day.
Memories start to haunt you
and you just can't get away.
Have you ever felt so lonely
the pain just seems to grow?
How much can you take
being such a lonely soul?
I can't really say because
I just don't really know.

Empty ship

I feel like an empty ship out at sea.
The waves are getting bigger
and I can hardly see.
The darkness slowly creeping in.
I'm silent but I want to scream.
The windows clouded with my doubt.
You can't see in and I can't see out.
I yearn to reach my safer shore.
I don't want to be scared or alone
anymore.

Disappear

Would it be better
if I could disappear?
Would it hurt less
if I wasn't here?
Every day I wake up
in a prison that I've made.
Maybe it's too late now
for me to be saved.
So much that I've
yet to see.
All my hopes and dreams.
Maybe they've passed me by
and now I'll never see.
If this is how it is now
and nothing is going to change,
I should just drift away
and finally, be okay.

Where do I belong?

I try so hard to find my way
but my fears consume me.
With every day that passes
by, I steadily start to lose me.
I've been alive years, yet
never really lived.
I feel with time I
have even less to give.
I'm a shadow on the wall.
A silent echo.
Is there better to come?
I really don't know.
I want to know love,
to be wanted for me.
Have a happy home,
start a family.
I want to feel safe and
I want to be strong.
If I can find love
I'd find where I belong.

Would I be remembered?

Would I be remembered
in the future when I'm gone?
Would I leave the world
glad that I had come?
Did I make a difference?
Leave it in a better place?
Did my life have meaning
or could I be replaced?
I hope I was good.
I hope I was kind,
went the extra mile.
I hope I made you smile
and showed you that I care.
Will you remember me
When I'm no longer here?
Will I be remembered
by my loved ones
when I'm gone?
I hope I am remembered
and my memory carries on.

I wish

I wish that I were better.
Better at being me.
I wish I could see the good
instead of the flaws I see.
I wish I could praise my journey
on just how far I've come.
Instead of focusing
on the things I haven't done.
I wish I could be kinder
to myself when times are hard.
Instead, I hurt and hate myself
adding to my scars.
I wish I could be better.
Treat myself with love.
But mostly I wish that I could feel
that I am good enough.

Find my way

I wander lost through clouds of doubt
hoping one day I'll find myself.
Lost in fear and insecurities will I
ever be happy being me?
Dreams and hope seemingly just out of
reach.
Time passing by yet I remain empty,
lost and hidden away.
Will there come a time?
Will I find my way?
I won't ever stop until I reach that day.
I won't give up on hope and I will find my way.

The forgotten

To the lonely souls
the world has misplaced.
Whose dreams have
disappeared.
Whose day is filled
with struggles and pain
that nobody can see.
To the hopeless and
the hurting with no
end in sight.
You are stronger than you
think you are.
Please don't give up the fight.
You may feel you are missing
and are the forgotten ones.
But I have faith in you as
I know how far you've come.

Lost soul

I hurt when you are hurting.
I sense and feel your pain.
I wish I knew a way that I
could take it all away.
I can see your sadness and
the trouble in your eyes.
I recognize another lost soul
as you pass me by.
You are not alone and there
are others just like you.
Feeling lost and forgotten
and not knowing what to do.
Things can and will get better
and I believe in you.
You will find your way and
the world will see you.

Nothing

I'm lost inside the darkness,
trapped inside a cage.
Hidden from the world outside,
alone inside my head.
Fear that's never ending,
that controls my every move.
So close to feeling that
I've nothing left to lose.
The pressure keeps on building
and soon I might implode.
But if I did and if I do
would anybody know?
I try so hard to fight it
with every single breath
but feel it won't be long
until I've nothing left.

Scared heart

My heart has been broken
and wounded many times.
It thinks itself worthy
then only to despise.
For if it was worthy
love surely it would find?
Instead I'm right back where I started
alone and wanting to hide.
My heart yearns for acceptance
and yearns to be enough.
It wants to be wanted
and it dreams of being loved.
My heart is beating,
that much is true.
But until it finds another heart
this just will not do.
My heart doesn't solely want
it has so much to give.
My heart would love with all its might
as long as it shall live.
It would take care of, love, respect and fight
for its love.
It would never forget
that love is a gift, a treasure to hold
on to and never let go.
My heart is fragile and so very scared
but I know it would be stronger
if it found someone who cared.

Lost

I must be lost.
I can't find my way.
Every step I take
I head the wrong way.
So many brick walls
and mountains to climb.
No matter the effort,
I get left behind.
I must be lost.
I don't know where to go.
I want to find my way
but the route I just don't know.
Every road I take
and every effort I make just
returns me to where I began
in my cold lost state.

Hiding behind a smile

I smile to hide my lonely soul,
so they can't see and they can't know.
For inside I'm empty, scared and afraid
and I can't let them see and I dare not explain.
I can't stand out as being seen
would open my wounds and then I shall bleed.
If I show weakness, they will know.
So I hide behind a smile and past me they will go.

The low

The emptiness hits me.
The low pulls me in.
I slip into a void.
Trying to claw my way out,
yet pulled further in by any attempt.
The light fades.
The darkness swallows me.
I feel helpless.
Trapped and alone.

Yet to come

We often focus on things we lack
or what we've yet to do.
We see all the negative but so
much positive is there too.
Yes, we have dreams and hope for
more but look at all you've done.
I see all your potential as I
know how far you've come.
Try to see all the little things
and the battles that you've won,
because I've no doubt there is
so much yet to come.

Climb

I've been at rock bottom.
I've clambered to the top.
I've fallen back down
but I will not stop.
I see a way out,
a goal,
an end.
So, I'll keep on climbing
until I make it
in the end.

The journey

The first step of any journey is
tentative when heading into the
unknown.
You must start walking if you want
to get where you need to go.
Each foot forward is significant, no
matter how big or small.
The journey is the lesson and your
destination the reward.

Strong

You think me weak
when I am strong.
You know not of
the battles I've won.
The mountains I've climbed
to get where I am.
Without wearing my shoes
you'd never understand.
Yes, I may be broken
but not beyond repair.
I'm stronger than you think
and in time I'll get there.
Please don't think me unworthy
because of the things I may lack.
They don't define me and
in time I'll change that.

Tomorrow

It's easy to get overwhelmed
by your insecurities.
To find yourself lost among
many of your fears.
To feel that you're not good enough and
that's what others will see.
To feel no sense of purpose
and that you're not worthy.
To feel misunderstood, disregarded
and not treated fairly.
To feel no one would notice
if you weren't there.
At times like these you must
remember that you aren't alone.
That these feelings are common
in lots of those you know.
That you are truly worthy
and always good enough.
To treat yourself with kindness
and with love.
Sometimes things seem bleak
and you cannot find your way
but there is always hope that
tomorrow will be a better day.

The past

Yesterday has been and gone.
Tomorrow has yet to come.
You can't change the past, nor
know what tomorrow may bring.
Focus on the here and now and
live each day like it's your last.
Live in the moment as it will
soon be in the past.

Never give up

Life isn't easy and sometimes seems too much.
When you try your best but it's never enough.
When things keep going wrong and you're in
despair, it's hard to believe the end is near.
Remember you've been here before and you
got through it then and know this difficult
time will end.
So, when you're feeling low and when it's
dark and you feel you've had enough, you
must remember to never give up.

Remember who you are

Don't ever feel you are all alone.
Don't ever feel you don't belong.
Don't hide away when you feel scared.
Don't listen to the bad things they've said.
Trust in who you are and keep reaching for the stars.
Look for the beauty in all you see.
Remember who you are.

I see you

I see you when you're lonely.
I see you when you're sad.
I see you when you're struggling
and when you're feeling bad.
I see you when you're hurting
and when you need a friend.
When you feel all alone,
I see you there my friend.

Take your pain away

I can see you're hurting.
I can sense your pain.
I wish there were something I could do
to take it all away.
I promise things can get better
and truly hope they do.
Just know that you are good enough
just by being you.
I want to see you smiling
and reaching all your dreams.
If I can ever help you know
you can always count on me.
You will get through this
and see brighter days.
I truly wish it were possible
to take your pain away.

Always

In the midst of darkness
always look for light.
When you see adversity
help with all your might.
Always act with kindness,
even to those who do wrong.
You don't know their story
or where they come from.
Think before you speak
as words are powerful.
Something you might say
could cause so much harm unknown.
Always be ready to listen to
someone who's in need.
It could be you one day when
help is so in need.
It takes less energy to smile
than it does to frown.
Greet the world with a smile
to all of those around.

The light

I look for the light
and my way out.
The tunnel seems
so long and dark.
My route is blocked
by fear and doubt.
I need to find the
light and my way out.
I want to scream for
help and someone to
find me.
I know the help I need
must come from me.
So, when lost in fear
and doubt I must be
the light and find my
own way out.

Depression

The light fades away
as you envelop me.
The path ahead and that
behind I can't see.
An empty hollowness
claws upon my chest.
I'm so exhausted yet
can never rest.
The silence and the racing thoughts
in equal measure deafen me.
I feel worthless, empty and devoid
of anything good.
What is wrong with me?
The darkness follows me
and it draws me in.
I want to let go and
I want to give in.
I feel so alone and
nobody can see that
slowly you're killing me.

Anxiety

Anxiety and stress.
Stress and anxiety.
Anxiety and stress.
So much inside I
need off my chest.
Everything spinning,
I'm sure I'll explode.
I don't think it's healthy
to carry this load.
Like the world on my shoulders,
a terrible weight.
This feeling inside
that I totally hate.
I hope I'll get through this
but fear that I can't.
I'll keep holding on
in the hope it will pass.

Hope

Hope is frail
it can be weak.
It can seem distant
to those who seek.
You may think it futile,
a waste of time but
hope keeps us going
and can keep us alive.
No matter how dark
things can seem.
Hold on to hope
and on to your dreams.

Back to the beginning

I wish I could go back
and try a different way.
Take back certain choices
and decisions that I made.
The years I've lost and
all that I've missed
just because I was scared.
I wish I had been stronger
and just didn't care.
If I had another chance,
I would want to begin again.
I would take risks and flirt
with hope.
I would jump headfirst
and not let go.
I would say what I needed
and fight for myself.
I would reach for my dreams
and never give up hope.

Distance

I want to see the world and
explore all its beauty.
Take in many cultures and
their history.
Meet people from so many
backgrounds and learn about
their lives.
See the hidden beauty that
the distance hides.

I hope

I hope you find your calling,
I hope you find your way.
I hope you find a way to smile
every single day.
I hope you find the strength
within to face all that you
need to.
I hope you find your worth
within and never let that go.
I hope you find friendship
wherever it may be.
I hope you find love and are
embraced by family.
I hope you find your happy
place and know that you belong.
I hope you find how special you
are and how so very strong.
I hope you find all of this and
so much more.
I believe in you and know this is
all possible.

Your impact

See the world with your heart,
not just your eyes.
Touch with your soul, not just
your person.
Listen with interest to learn
from all you hear.
Embrace with kindness and speak
with love.
Make a difference, find your
purpose and leave memories to be
proud.
Leave the world a better place
than that you found.

The human spirit

The human spirit is beautiful,
it has so much to give.
We all can make a difference
in how we choose to live.
Empathy, kindness and most
importantly love.
The world can never have enough.
Often through the darkest of times
people's humanity shines.
One's pain makes them not want others
to feel the way they do and if they
can make a difference they will.
That to me is humanity and the human
spirit in its greatest form.
For the human spirit to flourish then
hope and love must endure.

Friendship

In life there is still magic
if at times it's hard to see.
But when we look around
our friends are what we see.
When feeling lost,
when sad or hurt,
when just needing someone to talk to,
friends can lift us,
take the pain away.
Friendship is magic
in so many ways.
We choose our friends
and they choose us
and I believe
friendship is love.

Beauty

Beauty is all around us but when you
look you must see.
From the tiniest flower to the tallest
of trees.
The sound of birds singing and the
beautiful sky.
The sound of laughter and a stranger's
smile as they pass you by.
Kindness and giving and just doing right.
All beautiful things that give hope and
shine light.
So, look for the beauty wherever you are
and know you're a part of it because you
truly are.

The path

The path I walk upon
could tell such tales.
History woven into the
smallest of stones.
Echoes of the past that
linger with every step.
How many souls have
preceded me?
If the path could speak
of all who've passed, the tales would be endless
and the memories would last.
Imagine the many who've walked this path.

The girl from my dream

I met you whilst dreaming
and I'll never forget.
The feeling of belonging
and of content.
Our eyes met and I felt
your soul.
I knew then I'd never
let you go.
I held your hand as
we walked and laughed
and made plans that
I thought would last.
When I held you close
and I kissed your lips
it was like the sun had
vanished in an eclipse.
I was lost in the shade
that was all of you.
I had found my missing piece
and it was you.
Then suddenly you faded
and I would wake up.
I was alone again.
I knew it was a dream
but how could I forget
all that I had seen?

Everything I felt,
the sight and sound
of you.
I wanted to return to
my dream and return
to you.
I closed my eyes
and tried so hard
to drift back off to
sleep.
But I've never seen you
again, in any dream since.
You had forever gone
away from me.
I hope my dream was a foretelling
and one day we will truly meet.
I miss you now and always will,
the girl from my dream.

My missing piece

I feel your absence.
A missing part of me.
Someone and something I long for that has yet to be.
I yearn to be wanted, to be worthy of your love.
I dream of romance.
A future
A family too.
I seek all of this
and I'm searching for you.
I don't have much to offer
but I will give you all of me.
I just want to be good enough
and for you to come find me.
I want to feel what true love is.
To love and be loved too.
I need to find my missing piece.
I hope that soon I do.

Love

I'd love you like no other
and show you what love is.
Take away your worries with
every single kiss.
Hold you tight like treasure
and treat you preciously.
All your hopes and dreams will
be so important to me.
I'll protect you and all that
you hold dear.
Respect you in every way.
My love will surround you every
single day.
For me love is sacred and not
something you can throw away.
So, when I love I mean it and
that love is here to stay.

The beauty of words

Words to me are beauty.
Tools to convey meanings.
Sharing my thoughts that
I can never say.
They link us all together
and bind us like books.
Without words the world
could never be understood.

Why I write

I write from my heart and
will always be true.
All I want is to reach those
who need it to.
For others to feel like they're
no longer alone.
For my words to convey what they
can't say themselves.
I want to embrace them with kindness
and love and reassure them they're more
than good enough.
If I can help just one soul, then my
own battles I can endure because there
is nothing I want more.

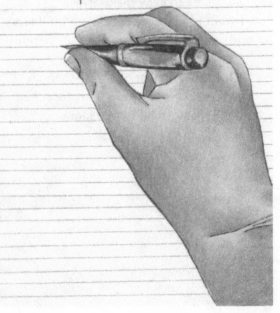

...for the human spirit to flourish
then hope and love must endure...

CPSIA information can be obtained
at www.ICGtesting.com
Printed in the USA
LVHW032113181121
703745LV00004B/96

9 781839 758553